Bridgestone
B O O K S

The Seven Continents

North America

Karen Bush Gibson

Consultant:
Mark Healy
Professor of Geography
William Rainey Harper College
Palatine, Illinois

Capstone
press

Mankato, Minnesota

Bridgestone Books are published by Capstone Press,
151 Good Counsel Drive, P.O. Box 669, Mankato, Minnesota 56002.
www.capstonepress.com

Library of Congress Cataloging-in-Publication Data
Gibson, Karen Bush.
    North America / Karen Bush Gibson.
    p. cm.—(Bridgestone books. The seven continents)
    Summary: "Describes the continent of North America, including climate, landforms, plants,
animals, countries, people, as well as North America and the world"—Provided by publisher.
    Includes bibliographical references and index.
    ISBN-13: 978-0-7368-5430-6 (hardcover)
    ISBN-10: 0-7368-5430-4 (hardcover)
    1. North America—Juvenile literature. 2. North America—Geography—Juvenile literature. I. Title.
II. Series: Seven continents (Mankato, Minn.)
E18.7.G53 2006
970—dc22   2005017260

Editorial Credits
Becky Viaene, editor; Patrick D. Dentinger, designer; Kim Brown and Tami Collins, map illustrators;
    Wanda Winch, photo researcher; Scott Thoms, photo editor

Photo Credits
Comstock, 12 (top right); Corbis/Bob Krist, 18 (left); Corbis/Lester Lefkowitz, 20; Corbis/Staffan
Widstrand, 6 (bottom right); Corbis/W. Perry Conway, cover (foreground); Corel, 12 (bottom);
Digital Vision, 6 (top, bottom left); Digital Vision/Joel Simon, 12 (top left); The Image Works/Andre
Jenny, 18 (right); The Image Works/Peter Hvizdak, 16; Map Resources, cover (background); Peter
Arnold, Inc./Martin Bond, 10; Photodisc/Sexto Sol/Adalberto Rios Szalay, 1

1 2 3 4 5 6 11 10 09 08 07 06

Table of Contents

Continents of the World

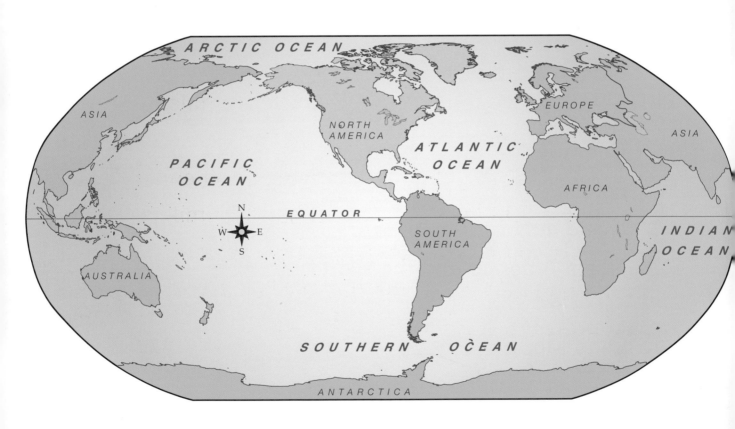

North America

The world's third largest continent covers some extreme ground. In North America, you can find everything from ice-covered islands to steamy **rain forests**. This huge landmass covers more than 9.3 million square miles (24.2 million square kilometers).

Most of the continent's people came in the last 400 years. Today, about 500 million people call North America home. What drew them? Part of the answer lies in the continent's variety.

◀ North America is connected to South America.

6

Climate

North America has every type of **climate**. Northern areas rarely get above freezing, while southern regions stay warm and wet all year. In between, much of this continent has four seasons. Cold winters give way to brisk springs. Then come warm summers and cool fall days.

Most of North America gets more than 10 inches (25 centimeters) of rain each year. Southern areas may get more, while **deserts** get much less.

◄ North America ranges from hot, dry deserts to cold icy land, but most of this continent has four seasons.

Landforms of North America

ARCTIC OCEAN

Bering Sea

Yukon River

Mt. Denali
20,320 feet
(6,194 meters)

Mackenzie River

Great Bear Lake

Great Slave Lake

Labrador Sea

Hudson Bay

PACIFIC OCEAN

Fraser River

Saskatchewan River

Nelson River

Lake Winnipeg

GREAT PLAINS

Snake River

ROCKY MOUNTAINS

Missouri River

Lake Superior

Lake Huron

St. Lawrence River

Lake Ontario

APPALACHIAN MOUNTAINS

Great Basin

Platte River

Mississippi River

Lake Michigan

Lake Erie

Colorado River

Arkansas River

Ohio River

Tennessee River

ATLANTIC OCEAN

Mississippi River

Rio Grande River

LEGEND

▲ Highest point

░ Mountains

⌒ River

Gulf of Mexico

Kilometers
0 200 400 600 800 1000

0 200 400 600
Miles

Caribbean Sea

8

SOUTH AMERICA

Landforms

Lakes, rivers, and mountains are found throughout North America. Lake Superior is the world's largest freshwater lake. Large amounts of water flow quickly in the long Mississippi River. Many other rivers flow into the Mississippi, coming from the Appalachian and Rocky Mountains.

Large deserts and plains cover parts of North America. Wind blows across the western Great Basin's dry land. East of the Rockies, **crops** grow on the Great Plains.

Plants

People use some of North America's plants when they read and sit down. Newspapers are made from trees that cover Canada and the northeastern United States. Mahogany trees from southern rain forests are used to make furniture.

Farmers plant many crops on this continent. About three-fifths of the world's soybeans grow in North America. Wheat, cotton, and fruit also grow there.

◄ Thick forests cover cool areas of upper North America.

Animals

Climate determines which animals can live in certain areas of North America. Polar bears and caribou live in the cold north. Jaguars hunt in the steamy, southern rain forests. Hot, dry North American deserts are home to **poisonous** Gila monsters. American bison roam the **temperate** Great Plains.

North America's waters are also full of life. Catfish, trout, and many other fish swim in lakes and rivers. Whales and sharks live in the oceans near North America.

◀ Thick fur warms polar bears, jaguars prowl in the rain forests, and Gila monsters brave the deserts' heat.

Countries of North America

ARCTIC OCEAN

GREENLAND (Denmark)

UNITED STATES (Alaska)

CANADA

PACIFIC OCEAN

UNITED STATES

ATLANTIC OCEAN

UNITED STATES (Hawaii)

MEXICO

THE BAHAMAS

HAITI

CUBA

DOMINICAN REPUBLIC

PUERTO RICO

ST. KITTS-NEVIS

JAMAICA

ANTIGUA & BARBUDA

BELIZE

DOMINICA

HONDURAS

GUATEMALA

ST. VINCENT & THE GRENADINES

ST. LUCIA

EL SALVADOR

NICARAGUA

GRENADA

BARBADOS

PANAMA

TRINIDAD & TOBAGO

COSTA RICA

N
W E
S

Kilometers
0   500   1000

0   620
Miles

14

SOUTH AMERICA

Countries

North America is made up of 23 countries and 14 territories. Canada is the largest country, but the United States has the most people. More than 293 million people live in the United States. North America's largest city, Mexico City, is home to more than 8 million people.

Thousands of islands are also part of North America. The world's largest island, Greenland, has long, cold winters. Islands in the Caribbean Sea have warm weather.

Population Density of North America

People per square mile		People per square kilometer
Less than 2		Less than 1
2 to 25		1 to 10
25 to 125		10 to 50
125 to 250		50 to 100
More than 250		More than 100

• **Major Cities/Urban Centers**
More than 7.5 million people

16

ARCTIC OCEAN

NORTH AMERICA

PACIFIC OCEAN

ATLANTIC OCEAN

New York

Los Angeles

Mexico City

SOUTH AMERICA

People

About 500 million people live in North America. More than 70 percent of them live in cities.

People move to North America from other continents, bringing hundreds of **cultures**, languages, and religions. Most North Americans speak English. Spanish is the second most used language, followed by French. The largest number of people are Christians, but Judaism and Islam also have many believers in North America.

◀ These school children (top) are part of the majority of North Americans that live in cities.

Living in North America

North American houses are different because of climate. Flat tile roofs keep houses cool in the warm south. In the north, melting snow drips off slanted roofs.

Climate also affects clothing. People in hot southern areas keep cool by wearing cotton clothing. During winter, people in northern areas wear coats and gloves.

People brought many new foods with them as they moved to North America. Today, North Americans enjoy food from around the world.

◄ Tile roofs keep southern houses cool. Farther north, people shovel snow off flat areas of roofs.

North America and the World

Much of the world buys North America's wood, food, minerals, and automobiles. This continent's forests provide large amounts of wood. North Americans also grow some of the world's food. Worldwide people buy North American minerals, such as copper, nickel, and silver. People also buy North American automobiles and parts.

Ships have carried tons of products away from this continent and millions of people to it. These people have shared their culture and helped shape this land.

◄ Giant rolls of paper, made from North America's large forests, are shipped to countries worldwide.

Glossary

climate (KLYE-mit)—the usual weather in a place

crop (KROP)—grain, fruit, or vegetables grown in large amounts that are often used for food

culture (KUHL-chur)—a people's way of life, ideas, art customs, and traditions

desert (DEZ-urt)—a very dry area of land; deserts receive less than 10 inches (25 centimeters) of rain each year.

poisonous (POI-zuhn-us)—able to harm with a poison called venom

rain forest (RAYN FOR-ist)—a tropical forest where much rain falls

temperate (TEM-pur-it)—having a mild climate, with neither very high nor very low temperatures

Read More

Striveildi, Cheryl. *North America.* A Buddy Book. Edina, Minn.: Abdo, 2003.

Vierow, Wendy. *North America.* Atlas of the Seven Continents. New York: PowerKids Press, 2004.

Internet Sites

FactHound offers a safe, fun way to find Internet sites related to this book. All of the sites on FactHound have been researched by our staff.

Here's how:
1. Visit *www.facthound.com*
2. Type in this special code **0736854304** for age-appropriate sites. Or enter a search word related to this book for a more general search.
3. Click on the **Fetch It** button.

FactHound will fetch the best sites for you!

Index